Thinking Critically:
Genetic Testing
and Research

Other titles in the *Thinking Critically* series include:

Thinking Critically: Genetic Testing and Research

Bradley Steffens

ReferencePoint Press®

San Diego, CA

© 2019 ReferencePoint Press, Inc.
Printed in the United States

For more information, contact:
ReferencePoint Press, Inc.
PO Box 27779
San Diego, CA 92198
www.ReferencePointPress.com

Picture Credits:
Cover: anyaivanova/Shutterstock.com
9: iStockphoto.com
Illustrations by Maury Aaseng

LIBRARY OF CONGRESS CATALOGING-IN-PUBLICATION DATA

Name: Steffens, Bradley, 1955– author.
Title: Thinking Critically: Genetic Testing and Research/by Bradley Steffens.
Description: San Diego, CA: ReferencePoint Press, Inc., 2019. | Series: Thinking Critically |
    Audience: Grade 9 to 12. | Includes bibliographical references and index.
Identifiers: LCCN 2018031462 (print) | LCCN 2018032379 (ebook) | ISBN 9781682825365 (ebook)
    | ISBN 9781682825358 (hardback)
Subjects: LCSH: Human chromosome abnormalities—Diagnosis. | Human chromosome
    abnormalities—Diagnosis—Moral and ethical aspects.
Classification: LCC RB155.6 (ebook) | LCC RB155.6 .S74 2019 (print) | DDC 616/.042—dc23
LC record available at https://lccn.loc.gov/2018031462

Contents

Foreword

"Literacy is the most basic currency of the knowledge economy we're living in today." Barack Obama (at the time a senator from Illinois) spoke these words during a 2005 speech before the American Library Association. One question raised by this statement is: What does it mean to be a literate person in the twenty-first century?

E.D. Hirsch Jr., author of *Cultural Literacy: What Every American Needs to Know*, answers the question this way: "To be culturally literate is to possess the basic information needed to thrive in the modern world. The breadth of the information is great, extending over the major domains of human activity from sports to science."

But literacy in the twenty-first century goes beyond the accumulation of knowledge gained through study and experience and expanded over time. Now more than ever literacy requires the ability to sift through and evaluate vast amounts of information and, as the authors of the Common Core State Standards state, to "demonstrate the cogent reasoning and use of evidence that is essential to both private deliberation and responsible citizenship in a democratic republic."

The *Thinking Critically* series challenges students to become discerning readers, to think independently, and to engage and develop their skills as critical thinkers. Through a narrative-driven, pro/con format, the series introduces students to the complex issues that dominate public discourse—topics such as gun control and violence, social networking, and medical marijuana. Each chapter revolves around a single, pointed question such as Can Stronger Gun Control Measures Prevent Mass Shootings?, or Does Social Networking Benefit Society?, or Should Medical Marijuana Be Legalized? This inquiry-based approach introduces student researchers to core issues and concerns on a given topic. Each chapter includes one part that argues the affirmative and one part that argues the negative—all written by a single author. With the single-author format the predominant arguments for and against an issue can be synthesized into clear, accessible discussions supported by details and evidence including relevant facts, direct quotes, current examples, and statistical illustrations. All volumes include focus questions to guide students as they read each pro/con discussion, a list of key facts, and an annotated list of related organizations and websites for conducting further research.

The authors of the Common Core State Standards have set out the particular qualities that a literate person in the twenty-first century must have. These include the ability to think independently, establish a base of knowledge across a wide range of subjects, engage in open-minded but discerning reading and listening, know how to use and evaluate evidence, and appreciate and understand diverse perspectives. The new *Thinking Critically* series supports these goals by providing a solid introduction to the study of pro/con issues.

Rearranging the Building Blocks of Life

The news for Milan and Elena Villarreal was devastating. Their newborn baby, Evelyn, had tested positive for a disease known as spinal muscular atrophy type 1 (SMA1). The Villarreals knew what the diagnosis meant: The muscles that enabled Evelyn to move and even to breathe would eventually cease to function. Her breathing would stop, and she would die. Evelyn's older sister Josephine had been born with the same disease and had died at age fifteen months. "We knew what we were dealing with," says Milan. "We'll love her for as long as we can."[1]

SMA1 is a genetic disease, transferred from parents to children through their genes, the chemical building blocks of life. Genes instruct the body's cells to make molecules called proteins that enable the cells and the entire body to function properly. Children with SMA1 lack a functioning SMN1 gene. This gene causes certain cells to produce a protein needed for the survival of spinal neurons. Spinal neurons transmit nerve impulses to the muscles, causing them to move. Without this protein, a child's spinal neurons cannot develop. As a result, the child's muscles atrophy until they no longer work.

The day that the Villarreals learned that Evelyn had SMA1, they searched the Internet to see if researchers had made any progress in the treatment of the disease since the death of Josephine. They found a clinic that was testing a way to send healthy SMN1 genes through the bloodstream and into the brain, where they are needed. At eight weeks old, Evelyn received the experimental treatment. Three years later, Evelyn is still alive, walking, talking, and even dancing. "It was just a miracle,"[2] says Milan.

The Science of Genetics

Evelyn's treatment and other similar treatments, known as gene therapy, are new and still experimental, but the science behind them is old. For thousands of years, farmers have known that breeding plants and animals with desirable traits often produces offspring with similar traits. They also found that crossbreeding two different but related kinds of plants or animals could produce offspring with the best traits from both breeds. Natural breeding has produced bigger and meatier cows, faster racehorses, larger and tastier fruits and vegetables, more beautiful flowers, and countless other agricultural wonders.

About 150 years ago an Austrian monk and scientist named Gregor Mendel discovered that an organism's traits are passed down from generation to generation in an orderly pattern. Mendel theorized that inherited traits are governed by unseen biological mechanisms that he called factors. In 1905 Danish botanist Wilhelm Johannsen named

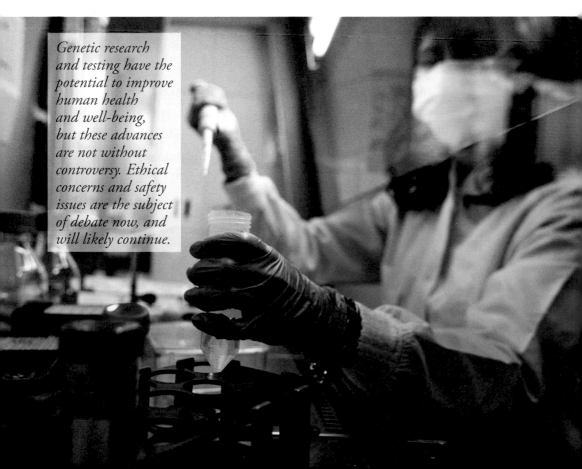

Genetic research and testing have the potential to improve human health and well-being, but these advances are not without controversy. Ethical concerns and safety issues are the subject of debate now, and will likely continue.

these factors genes, after the Greek word *gonos*, meaning "offspring" and "procreation." Six years later, American biologist Thomas Hunt Morgan determined that the material containing genes resides in microscopic structures in a cell's nucleus called chromosomes. Morgan was studying fruit flies, which have eight chromosomes. Later scientists learned that humans have forty-six chromosomes, arranged in twenty-three pairs inside the cell nucleus.

Scientists still did not know which materials conveyed the hereditary information, since chromosomes contain proteins and other molecules. Most scientists thought that proteins did the work, but in 1952 American geneticists Alfred Hershey and Martha Chase showed that a molecule known as deoxyribonucleic acid (DNA) governed inheritance. A year later American biologist James Watson and English physicist Francis Crick discovered that DNA molecules are composed of two threadlike structures wound around each other in the shape of a helix. This structure allows the DNA molecules to divide and make copies of themselves as cells divide, transmitting the hereditary information to each new cell. Each chromosome is made up of a DNA molecule tightly wound many times around proteins that support its structure.

Genes are relatively short sections of DNA molecules. DNA also contains vast amounts of noncoding material. In fact, the more than twenty-one thousand protein-coding genes in the forty-six chromosomes make up less than 2 percent of a cell's total genetic material, known collectively as the human genome. Not all genomes are perfect. As cells divide and organisms grow, mutations can occur in the genome. Occasionally, genes are missing or malformed. These mutations can cause genetic diseases. Scientists realized that if they could repair or replace these genes, they might be able to prevent or cure genetic diseases. This is the basis of gene therapy.

The Human Genome Project

As geneticists learned where certain genes are located on the DNA strands, it became clear that it would be ideal to locate all the human genes. That way scientists would better understand the sources of both healthy traits and genetic diseases. In 1988 the US Congress authorized spending for a project to sequence the human genome. American scientists were joined by scientists from around the world in what became known as the Human Genome Project. In 2003 the project's researchers completed their work. Francis S. Collins, a physician and scientist who served as the project's director, describes his hopes for what the Human Genome Project would help accomplish: "For me, as a physician, the true payoff from the HGP [Human Genome Project] will be the ability to better diagnose, treat, and prevent disease, and most of those benefits to humanity still lie ahead. With these immense data sets of sequence and variation now in hand, we are now empowered to pursue those goals in ways undreamed of a few years ago."[3]

> "The true payoff from the HGP [Human Genome Project] will be the ability to better diagnose, treat, and prevent disease, and most of those benefits to humanity still lie ahead."[3]
>
> —Francis S. Collins, director of the Human Genome Project

A Medical Revolution

Collins's vision is coming true. Gene therapy techniques have been developed to treat not only SMA1 but also HIV-AIDS, cystic fibrosis, rheumatoid arthritis, hemophilia B, and several kinds of cancer. So far, however, the US Food and Drug Administration (FDA), the federal agency that oversees the introduction of drugs and medical therapies, has only approved two gene therapies for general use in the United States. One treats acute cancer of the blood in pediatric and young adult patients, and the other treats an inherited form of vision loss that may result in blindness. Several other gene therapies are on track to be approved as well. "I believe gene therapy will become a mainstay in treating, and maybe curing, many of our most devastating and intractable illnesses,"[4] says FDA commissioner Scott Gottlieb.

Gene therapy received an important boost in 2013 when researchers at the Massachusetts Institute of Technology and Harvard University edited human DNA using a system known as CRISPR-Cas9. Based on the way that bacteria capture snippets of DNA from invading viruses, CRISPR-Cas9 is able to snip DNA like a pair of scissors at a targeted location. Once the DNA is cut, genetic engineers can add or delete genetic material at a precise location. "The CRISPR-Cas9 system has generated a lot of excitement in the scientific community because it is faster, cheaper, more accurate, and more efficient than other existing genome editing methods,"[5] states the National Institutes of Health (NIH).

Uses of DNA

Knowledge of the human genome is being used for far more than medical treatments. Since sections of DNA vary from person to person, DNA profiles can be used to identify people. For example, by comparing a person's DNA to that found at a crime scene, law enforcement investigators can determine if a person is linked to a crime. Similarly, if a person's DNA does not match the DNA at a crime scene, that person can be ruled out as a suspect. DNA evidence is used both to convict criminals and to free people wrongly convicted of crimes.

> "I believe gene therapy will become a mainstay in treating, and maybe curing, many of our most devastating and intractable illnesses."[4]
>
> —Scott Gottlieb, FDA commissioner

DNA comparisons can also determine if two people are related. For example, DNA testing can be used to determine if a man is (or is not) the biological father of a child when there is doubt about a child's paternity. Genetic testing can also identify distant relatives and, through them, common ancestors. As a result, genetic testing has become a useful tool in genealogical research. Genetic testing has become so commonplace that companies now sell home genetic testing kits that are used to collect DNA samples, usually from saliva. Some companies test only for genealogical information, but others also look for mutated genes that are linked to genetic diseases. As of August 2018 more than 15 million Americans had taken at-home genetic tests.

Genetically Modified Organisms

All living things—plants, animals, and microorganisms—have a genome, and scientists study them as well. Scientists have learned what proteins certain plant and animal genes express, and they have experimented with altering those genes to bring out desirable characteristics. These are known as genetically modified organisms. For example, the genes of some laboratory mice have been edited to make them better specimens for studying certain diseases. Similarly, the genes of certain food crops have been altered to make them resistant to pests, diseases, and pesticides. Many of these genetically modified foods have been approved by the FDA for human consumption.

Genetic research is bringing about many changes that can improve human health and well-being. However, some of these changes raise ethical issues about how far genetic changes should go and who should decide what the limits will be. Other changes raise health and safety concerns. These issues are sure to be debated for many years to come.

Chapter One

Is Genetic Engineering Ethical?

Genetic Engineering Is Not Ethical

- Genetic engineering may have unforeseen negative consequences.
- Changing the human genome will affect future generations without their consent.
- It is unclear who should decide which genetic changes are beneficial and which are not.

The Debate at a Glance

Genetic Engineering Is Ethical

- Eradicating genetic diseases and human suffering is not only ethical but a moral duty.
- There is nothing unethical about giving prospective parents the ability to bring healthy children into the world
- Germline editing can be performed safely.

Genetic Engineering Is Not Ethical

"Genome editing in human embryos using current technologies could have unpredictable effects on future generations. This makes it dangerous and ethically unacceptable."

—Edward Lanphier, president and chief executive officer of Sangamo BioSciences and chair of the Alliance for Regenerative Medicine

Edward Lanphier et al., "Don't Edit the Human Germ Line," *Nature*, March 12, 2015. www.nature.com.

Consider these questions as you read:

1. In scientific research, how much attention should be paid to concerns about unforeseen consequences? Explain your answer.
2. Do you think eliminating embryos and fetuses with genetic defects is ethical? Why or why not?
3. Do you think it is ethical to do something that affects future generations without their consent? Explain your answer.

Editor's note: The discussion that follows presents common arguments made in support of this perspective, reinforced by facts, quotes, and examples taken from various sources.

In 2015 a team of researchers led by Junjiu Huang, a genetic researcher at Sun Yat-sen University in Guangzhou, China, used CRISPR-Cas9 technology to edit the genome of a single-cell fertilized human embryo. In theory, as the cells divided and the embryo developed, the altered gene would be present in all of the embryo's future cells (including reproductive cells). And these altered genes would be passed on to later generations—which could mean the elimination of inherited diseases.

Some scientists hail this activity as a leap forward for medicine. Others are not so sure. Editing the genetic material passed down to future generations, known as the germline, raises serious ethical issues. Foremost

15

among these issues are questions relating to what limits should be placed on such changes and who should make these decisions. These issues are so unsettled that fifteen European nations prohibit germline editing research. Experimentation is legal in the United States, but the NIH refuses to fund it. This does not go far enough. It is time for the United States and all nations to ban such research.

Dangerous Side Effects

One of the most serious dangers posed by germline editing is that it could introduce unplanned changes in a person's genome, known as off-target effects. Those changes could then be passed down to that person's descendants, just as naturally occurring genetic diseases are now. Off-target effects have already happened in more traditional gene therapy. For example, in 2000 twenty young patients in France received gene therapy for a severe immune deficiency. The inserted genes missed their targets in five of the patients. These genes entered the patients' genomes at places that caused the cells to become cancerous. The cells divided and grew, and all five patients died from leukemia—cancer of the blood. Editing the germline could bring about similar terrible results. Off-target effects could cause known cancers and genetic diseases, but they could also introduce new diseases.

The problem is that no one would know about the off-target effects until the child whose genes were edited was born and developed symptoms. In fact, the disease might not show up in the first person with the off-target effects at all. Many genetic diseases only develop if a child receives mutated genes from both parents. It could be that germline changes would only cause a disease in the descendants of the person who received the treatment. By the time the off-target effects are discovered, they could already be in the genes of many people. This is why many scientists believe germline editing is unpredictable and unethical.

The human germline editing conducted so far suggests that off-target effects are likely. Huang's original study found a large number of off-target effects—more than have been reported in gene-editing studies of mouse embryos or human adult cells. Huang admits that the number of

Americans Are Concerned About Germline Editing

Americans are more reluctant to accept gene editing when it could affect future generations than they are when it affects only a single patient, according to a Pew Research Center survey. About half of adults say gene editing would be less acceptable to them if the effects changed the genetic makeup of the whole population, as germline editing would. Only 23 percent find gene editing less acceptable when it is limited to a single person.

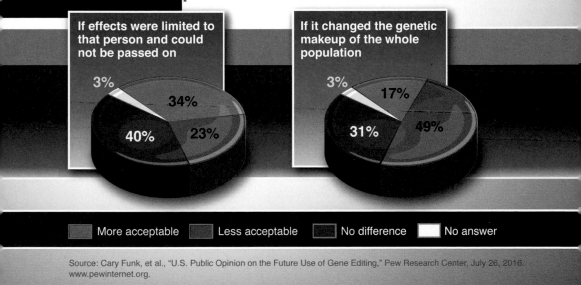

% of US adults who say gene editing giving healthy babies a much reduced risk of serious diseases would be more acceptable, less acceptable, or make no difference . . .

If effects were limited to that person and could not be passed on

3%   34%   40%   23%

If it changed the genetic makeup of the whole population

3%   17%   31%   49%

More acceptable   Less acceptable   No difference   No answer

Source: Cary Funk, et al., "U.S. Public Opinion on the Future Use of Gene Editing," Pew Research Center, July 26, 2016. www.pewinternet.org.

off-target effects was likely even higher than reported because his team only examined part of the genome. "If we did the whole genome sequence, we would get many more,"[6] Huang says. Huang's research shows that the danger of off-target effects is real. Given this reality, to continue this research is highly unethical.

A Matter of Consent

Unintended consequences are not the only reason that genetic engineering is unethical. Normally, before a medical procedure or treatment is started, the doctor fully explains the procedure or treatment to the patient. The patient then decides whether to move forward. By giving consent, the patient states that he or she understands the possible risks associated with the proposed actions. In the case of germline editing (a process that involves changes being made in an embryo), parents make that decision for themselves and on behalf of the child they hope to bear from that embryo. The child and his or her future descendants will have no say in the matter. From an ethics perspective, this is shaky ground. "The individuals whose lives are potentially affected by germline manipulation could extend many generations into the future," writes Francis S. Collins, director of the NIH and former director of the Human Genome project. "They can't give consent to having their genomes altered from what nature would have made possible."[7]

Nonmedical Changes

Even if germline editing for disease is proved 100 percent safe and effective, the process raises other ethical issues regarding which conditions will be treated. While no rational person would argue that having a deadly inherited disease such as cystic fibrosis is a good thing, the same cannot be said for inherited conditions such as dwarfism or blindness. People who were born blind, for instance, can and do become fully contributing members of society. Their lives have as much value as the lives of sighted people. Yet if genetic engineering (and especially techniques like germline editing) were to become routine, these people would likely disappear and their unique perspectives and contributions would be lost. "Where do you draw the line?"

"At what point are we engaging in eugenics and not accepting the normal diversity within a population?"[8]

—Mark A. Rothstein, director of the Institute for Bioethics at the University of Louisville School of Medicine

18

asks Mark A. Rothstein, director of the Institute for Bioethics at the University of Louisville School of Medicine. "On the one hand we have to view . . . [genetic engineering] as a positive in terms of preventing disability and illness. But at what point are we engaging in eugenics and not accepting the normal diversity within a population?"[8]

If inherited disabilities can be eliminated with germline editing, the question becomes, what is a disability? "In which category would we put short stature, for example?" asks Marcy Darnovsky, the executive director of the Center for Genetics and Society. "We know that taller people tend to earn more money. So do people with paler skins. Should arranging for children with financially or socially 'efficient' varieties of height and complexion be considered medical intervention?"[9] This is a serious question. If germline editing for diseases and disabilities becomes commonplace, it would only be a matter of time before there was demand to use it for creating people with specific characteristics. That is not the purpose of medicine, and it would be unethical to open the door to the possibility of it occurring.

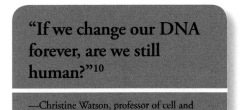

"If we change our DNA forever, are we still human?"[10]

—Christine Watson, professor of cell and cancer biology at Cambridge University

Who Decides?

Germline editing raises ethical questions that are broader and more intricate than those posed by any previous medical technology. It is the first technology that will affect not only the patient being treated but all of that patient's descendants. If germline editing is adopted on a large scale, human beings will replace nature as the guiding force of human evolution. Christine Watson, a professor of cell and cancer biology at Cambridge University, asks, "If we change our DNA forever, are we still human?"[10] The current code of medical ethics is not prepared to answer such a question. Current ethics would leave questions of germline editing in the hands of prospective parents, whose concern is with their own child, not with the fate of the human species. The doctors or the scientists involved will be aware of the broader implications, but they will also be guided by current ethics, which focus on the well-being of the patient. They will also believe they are helping cure a genetic disease in the patient's family and thus playing a part in wiping it out. Curing disease is the goal of medicine, and their considerations will likely end there. Governmental leaders could step in and decide what changes are permissible, but they are not experts in science or ethics. In addition, they have their own interests. They might see germline editing as a way of saving the government from future health care costs. Besides, their decisions are binding only in their own country. The world could end up with a patchwork of policies, some of which would allow germline editing to proceed. What is needed is a global conversation that involves not just parents, doctors, and scientists, but also ethicists, philosophers, and religious leaders. Germline editing must be stopped until these ethical issues are resolved in a rational way.

Genetic Engineering Is Ethical

"If we could use gene editing to remove the gene sequences in an embryo that cause sickle cell disease or cystic fibrosis, I would say not only that we may do so, but in the case of such severe diseases, that we have a moral obligation to do so."

—Ronald M. Green, professor emeritus of religion and ethics at Dartmouth College

Ronald M. Green, "Do We Have a Moral Obligation to Genetically Enhance Our Children?," Hastings Center, October 31, 2017. www.thehastingscenter.org.

Consider these questions as you read:

1. What are the social and ethical responsibilities of the scientific community toward present-day society and future generations?
2. If it were possible for all prospective parents to select a healthy embryo over one that has a potentially harmful genetic mutation, would this be ethical? Why or why not?
3. What criteria should be used to determine whether or not to do germline editing?

Editor's note: The discussion that follows presents common arguments made in support of this perspective, reinforced by facts, quotes, and examples taken from various sources.

The world celebrated when the World Health Organization declared that the smallpox virus, which had claimed millions of lives over human history, was eradicated in 1980. It was the first deadly disease to have been completely wiped out using scientific knowledge, first by identifying the cause of the disease and then by taking preventive steps to stop its spread using widespread inoculation. It was also a triumph of public health care policy, as the nations of the world united to vaccinate entire populations against the scourge and identify and isolate the last remaining pockets of the disease. Genetic engineers are now on track to prevent other devastating diseases. In this case, eradication will come not through vaccination, but through comprehensive prenatal genetic screening and germline editing. Using genetic engineering, scientists will eventually be able to wipe out deadly hereditary diseases such as cystic fibrosis, sickle-cell anemia, and Tay-Sachs disease.

From the beginning of medical history, the goal has been to ease and prevent human suffering. Genetic engineering represents the most recent development in those laudable efforts. And it promises some important outcomes. "In the distant future, I could imagine that altered germ lines would protect humans against cancer, diabetes and other age-related problems,"[11] says Nobel Prize–winning geneticist Craig Mello of the University of Massachusetts–Worcester. If the medical community has the means to prevent disease and suffering, it has a moral and ethical obligation to do so.

The Right of Consent

Some people argue that changing the human genome is unethical because it affects future generations without their consent. The problem with this argument is that it confers rights on people who do not exist, and then it says we cannot violate those rights. These imaginary people and their imaginary rights are not considered in any other human activity. One does not need the permission of the unborn to drive a car, yet automobile accidents are the leading cause of accidental death, and accidental deaths affect the unborn. More to the point, one does not need the permission of the unborn to have an abortion, even though abortions terminate the lives of the unborn and all of their potential descendants. The idea that nonexistent people have rights is absurd.

In the case of germline editing, the parents and their doctors would bear

"In the distant future, I could imagine that altered germ lines would protect humans against cancer, diabetes and other age-related problems."[11]

—Nobel Prize–winning geneticist Craig Mello of the University of Massachusetts–Worcester

Two-Thirds of Americans Support Germline Editing

Two-thirds of Americans find gene editing acceptable if it is used for medical therapy, regardless of whether it is limited to individuals (somatic therapy) or passed down to future generations (germline therapy). According to a study by researchers at the University of Wisconsin–Madison, 63.6 percent of adults surveyed found somatic therapy acceptable and 64.9 percent found germline therapy acceptable.

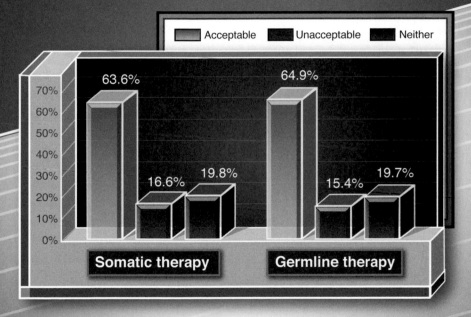

Source: Alessandra Potenza, "Two-Thirds of Americans Approve of Editing Human DNA to Treat Disease," The Verge, August 30, 2017. www.theverge.com.

the responsibility of consent. This is as it should be. It is similar to when prospective parents who use in vitro fertilization (IVF) to conceive decide which embryo to implant for a successful birth. Editing the genes of a fertilized egg before transferring it into the woman's body would simply be an extension of this process—done with the aim of ensuring the health of the new life. There is nothing unethical about giving prospective parents the ability to bring healthy children into the world.

Parents already make life-and-death decisions that affect their children and their future children. For example, many IVF patients choose to have their developing embryos tested for genetic diseases before being transferred to the woman's body. This is known as preimplantation genetic testing (PGT). If PGT shows that one of the embryos a couple is considering for implantation has a genetic disease and another embryo does not, the couple has the right to implant the healthy embryo and discard the unhealthy one. This power over the life and death of the embryos resides with the parents—as it should. Choosing embryos for implantation is in some ways a more momentous decision than whether to repair a single-cell embryo with germline editing, and it is considered ethical. Repairing the cell before implantation is ethical as well.

Many couples cannot produce an embryo that does not have a genetic disease, because of their genetic makeup. Many such couples forgo having biological children, opting either to have no children at all or to adopt. With germline editing, such couples can have a disease-causing gene repaired. This not only would allow the couple to have their own biological children without passing on the genetic disease, it would ensure that the child's descendants are also free of disease. Deciding to do so is ethical and within the scope of parental decision making.

Safeguarding Patient Safety

Safety is paramount in any research that involves human health and human life. It would be highly unethical to introduce new diseases into the human species or even to introduce treatments that cause more harm than good. No one wants to repeat the mistake of the 1950s, when doctors prescribed a sedative known as thalidomide to pregnant women to alleviate nausea and morning sickness, only to find out later that the drug caused malformations in the limbs of more than five thousand babies born to those women. Scientists who work in the field of germline editing are well aware that off-target changes to the human genome could produce equally harmful and possibly worse effects, and they are working to make sure that their research does not go awry. "Do no harm" remains an important part of medical ethics.

A team led by Shoukhrat Mitalipov at Oregon Health & Science University (OHSU) is adhering to that principle. It performed gene editing on 163 human embryos and reported no off-target effects. None of these embryos were implanted, because the researchers know that more testing must be done before that step is taken. However, Mitalipov's team did not have to wait for the implantation of an embryo or the birth of a child to say with confidence that there were no off-target effects. That is because Mitalipov and his team were able to sequence the genomes of the repaired embryos and compare them to normal genomes to see if there were any misplaced or mutated genes. They reported that there were not. If there are no off-target effects in the genome of an embryo, there can be no off-target effects in the child that develops from that embryo, since the genome is copied exactly every time a cell divides. If no off-target effects can occur, no harm can be done.

If off-target effects were to occur during germline editing, they would be found in PGT, just as natural mutations and diseases are today. PGT is how Huang and other human germline researchers have found that their germline editing did create off-target effects. Were doctors to find embryos with off-target effects after germline editing, those embryos would be not be implanted. They would be discarded, just as diseased embryos are today. As a result, no new mutations or diseases would be introduced to the human germline. PGT will ensure that human germline editing is safe and therefore ethical.

Critics of germline editing are not opposed to using gene therapy on newborns, but they are opposed to its use on embryos before implantation. This makes no sense. The process is the same in both cases. If anything, it is more ethical to treat the genetic disease in a single cell before implantation than to wait until a diseased child is born, when more cells have to be treated and the risks of off-target effects are higher.

> "I didn't do this research to satisfy my curiosity. This was done to develop the technology and bring it to clinics."[12]
>
> —Shoukhrat Mitalipov, head of the Center for Embryonic Cell and Gene Therapy at OHSU

In addition, germline editing will not only prevent the genetic disease in the child that develops, it also will free that child from worry about passing on a genetic disease to his or her descendants.

Germline editing is proceeding without the support of the NIH. For example, Mitalipov is conducting germline research on viable embryos using OHSU's institutional funds and grants from charitable foundations. It is only a matter of time until a child treated with germline editing is born. "I didn't do this research to satisfy my curiosity," Mitalipov says. "This was done to develop the technology and bring it to clinics."[12] The NIH's head-in-the-sand approach to germline editing is shortsighted. The ethical thing to do is to support such research to make sure it is done safely.

Chapter Two

Is Genetic Testing Beneficial?

Genetic Testing Is Beneficial

- Genetic testing can ease concerns about developing a disease or allow individuals to get medical help early.
- Doctors can use genetic testing to determine personalized treatment plans for their patients.
- People who learn they are at risk for developing a genetic disease may be able to prevent onset of that disease by changing their diet and lifestyle.

The Debate at a Glance

Genetic Testing Is Harmful

- Discovering possible future disorders that cannot be treated or cured can create unnecessary fear and stress.
- Genetic testing can give a false sense of security, leading a person to make unhealthy choices.
- Genetic testing can reveal secrets relating to adoptions or paternity that can create problems and stress within a family.

Genetic Testing Is Beneficial

"By using genetics, you can help some people prevent or interrupt something at an earlier stage where the costs are much lower."

—Othman Laraki, chief executive of Color Genomics, a genetic testing firm

Quoted in Natasha Singer, "Employees Jump at Genetic Testing. Is That a Good Thing?," *New York Times*, April 15, 2018. www.nytimes.com.

Consider these questions as you read:

1. Would you want to know if you have a gene that causes a genetic disease? Why or why not?
2. What are the benefits of learning that a person is at risk of developing a genetic disease? What are the drawbacks?
3. Do you believe genetic screening should become a standard part of medical care? Why or why not?

Editor's note: The discussion that follows presents common arguments made in support of this perspective, reinforced by facts, quotes, and examples taken from various sources.

Each person has a story written into his or her body. It is the story of the person's ancestors. It is also a story of the person's health and whether he or she might develop a disease passed down through the generations. These stories are written into each person's genetic code, the arrangement of chemical building blocks that determine physical characteristics. Until recently, these stories were impossible to read. But with the sequencing of the human genome and the development of high-speed DNA sequencers, which can identify which genes a person has and where they are located on a strand of DNA, virtually anyone can learn what is written into his or her genetic code.

Medical Benefits

Genetic testing can help people who have a family history of an inherited disease. Their parents, grandparents, or great-grandparents may have died from the disease. For example, Huntington's disease is a deadly degenerative disease that can be inherited. Children of someone with Huntington's disease have a 50 percent chance of inheriting the gene that causes the disease. Before genetic testing, such children might spend many years of their lives wondering if they would develop the disease. With genetic testing, people can find out for certain if they carry the gene for the disease. Finding out that they do not carry the gene can provide an immense sense of relief, reducing stress and enhancing people's well-being for many years.

Even those who find out they do have a disease-causing gene can benefit from having this information. They can immediately begin working with doctors and other health professionals to develop a plan for the years ahead. For instance, patients and doctors can watch for early signs of illness and begin treatment as soon as the first signs of the disease develop. New Yorker Ann Mellinger had no known family history of breast, ovarian, or prostate cancer, but she nevertheless took a test from 23andMe—one of the companies that offers at-home genetic testing. She wanted to find out if she had the BRCA1 and BRCA2 genes associated with increased risk for breast, ovarian, and prostate cancer. "Most people who test positive for the BRCA1 mutation have a family history of breast and ovarian cancer, but I was aware of no cases in our family," says Mellinger. Nevertheless, the test showed that she has one of the cancer-related genes. "Knowledge is power," says Mellinger, "and in my case, the information I gained could quite possibly have saved my life."[13]

> "Knowledge is power, and in my case, the information I gained could quite possibly have saved my life."[13]
>
> —Ann Mellinger, a corporate executive and genetic testing consumer

Some people do not have symptoms of a genetic disease, but they may carry a mutated gene that is linked to disease. As a result, they might pass on the mutated gene on to their children. These people are known as genetic disease carriers. Their children in turn may develop the disease or become carriers themselves. Genetic testing can reveal if the person is a carrier. This knowledge can help people make informed choices about whether to have a baby. Sara Faye Green, a writer for *Women's Health* magazine, found out from a home genetic test that she was a carrier of Gaucher's disease, an inherited disorder that affects many of the body's organs and tissues. She writes, "I'm glad to know that I'm a carrier of a genetic disease so I can plan against the risk and make choices for myself and my future with the most knowledge possible."[14]

Personalized Medicine

Genetic tests can also reveal which drugs can be most effective for treatments. Right now, most drugs are approved for use by everyone—a one-size-fits-all approach. However, scientists have learned that a person's genetic makeup can affect how he or she responds to medications. As a result, treatment can be tailored to the individual's genetic makeup. This is known as personalized medicine. Jyoti Patel, a cancer physician and professor of medicine at the University of Chicago, explains:

> Genetic testing has really changed our approach to cancer. . . . We've made significant progress over the past decade of really cataloging some of the genetic changes that we see when cancer occurs. So there are particular mutations that may make someone more susceptible to developing cancer, there are other mutations that when detected in the tumor, cause a dysfunction of a particular protein for which we've developed drugs.[15]

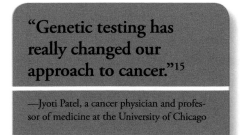

"Genetic testing has really changed our approach to cancer."[15]

—Jyoti Patel, a cancer physician and professor of medicine at the University of Chicago

Not only can genetic testing help doctors choose better treatments, it can warn them away from potentially harmful ones. "If doctors know your genes, they can predict drug response and incorporate this

Millions Find At-Home Genetic Testing Useful

The number of people taking at-home genetic tests grew astronomically between 2013 and 2018, with the number of users nearly tripling from 4 million to more than 12 million from 2017 to 2018 alone. The growing popularity of genetic testing shows that consumers find it useful and beneficial.

Total number of people tested by consumer genetics companies, in millions

Ancestry DNA only
All major testing companies

12M
10M
8M
6M
4M
2M
0M

2013   2014   2015   2016   2017   2018

Source: Antonio Regalado, "2017 Was the Year Consumer DNA Testing Blew Up," *MIT Technology Review*, February 12, 2018. www.technologyreview.com.

information into the medical decisions they make," says Rochelle Long, an expert in the interaction of drugs and genetic makeups at the NIH. "By screening to know who shouldn't get certain drugs, we can prevent life-threatening side effects."[16]

Sometimes genetic screening reveals that the optimum therapy for a person is not a drug but gene therapy. For example, some people have genes that do not produce sufficient amounts of lipoprotein lipase. This protein breaks down large fat-carrying particles that circulate in the blood after each meal. Without this protein, the particles can obstruct small blood vessels, causing an inflammation of the pancreas, called pancreatitis. If individuals learn through genetic testing that they have this gene, they can seek a gene therapy called Glybera that has been approved for use by the European Medicines Agency. As more gene therapies come online, genetic testing will become commonplace, because people will know their disease-causing genes can be repaired or replaced.

Healthy Lifestyles

Medications and gene therapy are not the only things that can be tailored to a person's genetic makeup to improve outcomes. The same principle applies to diet and exercise. Just as there is an individual reaction to drugs based on a person's genes, so too is there an individual reaction to foods and exercises. As a result, companies like DNAFit, Habit, Kinetic Diagnostics, and Simplified Genetics now offer direct-to-consumer genetic testing kits for fitness and nutrition counseling. For example, Jen Judson, a reporter in Arlington, Virginia, found that the standard weight-loss recommendation of eating less and exercising more was not helping her control her weight. She took an at-home genetic test to see if it would reveal any answers. The testing company found that Judson's body does not process carbohydrates very efficiently. It recommended that she lower her carb intake and eat more protein and healthy fats. The test also suggested that she burns half as many calories during exercise as someone with normal metabolism does. The results did not surprise Judson. "I really already knew what I needed to do and how my body responded to certain foods,"[17] she says. Still, she was glad to learn the genetic cause behind what she had observed.

Sometimes a genetic test might show that a person carries a gene that makes developing a disease more likely but not a certainty. For example, a person might have a gene that indicates he or she is at risk for obesity or type 2 diabetes. However, that person can make lifestyle choices regarding diet and exercise that minimize that risk. In this way, genetic testing can motivate people to make better choices and lead healthier lives. This is the thinking behind a program pioneered by Geisinger Health System, a Pennsylvania-based health care system. Geisinger has begun offering genetic screening to its patients, with the goal of testing all 3 million of them. The test looks for mutations in more than seventy-five genes that are associated with dozens of medical conditions, including heart disease and cancer. Geisinger then counsels the patients who test positive for a disease, telling them what they can do to prevent or forestall the diseases. "Geisinger is prescribing DNA sequencing to patients and putting DNA results in electronic health records and actually creating an action plan to prevent that predisposition from occurring," says Wendy Wilson, a Geisinger spokesperson. "We are preventing disease from happening."[18]

Genetic testing is revolutionizing medicine, making both preventive care and the treatment of disease more effective. Even so, genetic-based medicine is still in its infancy. There are even better things to come.

Genetic Testing Is Harmful

"The hype and excitement about mail-order genetic testing is understandable. But when technologies have the potential to generate harm to individuals and society, with minimal evidence of compensating benefits, it is fair to require that a better case be made for their permissibility and adoption."

—Daniel Munro, professor of ethics at the University of Ottawa's Graduate School of Public and International Affairs, Ottawa, Canada

Daniel Munro, "The Dangers of Mail-In Genetic Testing," *Maclean's*, June 5, 2017. www.macleans.ca.

Consider these questions as you read:

1. In what ways can at-home genetic testing be beneficial? In what ways can it be harmful?
2. Do you think people should be required to meet with a genetic counselor when they receive the results of at-home genetic testing? Why or why not?
3. Do you believe at-home genetic testing should be regulated? Explain your answer.

Editor's note: The discussion that follows presents common arguments made in support of this perspective, reinforced by facts, quotes, and examples taken from various sources.

Several companies now offer at-home genetic testing kits so consumers can learn about their genealogy and their genetic disease profile. The companies providing these services often tell heartwarming stories of family reunions that resulted from clients who found genetic matches in the companies' databases. They also offer testimonials from people who were able to seek lifesaving treatment for genetic diseases. These companies are not required to discuss the dark side of at-home genetic testing, but there is one. Genetic testing can expose family secrets that have been carefully guarded out of concern and even love for those involved. These tests can also reveal the presence of genetic disease risks that can menace a person's thoughts without the disease necessarily developing. Hurt, anger, fear, and depression—these can be the unforeseen consequences of at-home genetic testing.

Unpredictable Outcomes

Genetic testing can reveal that a person carries a mutant gene linked to a genetic disease. Genetic testing companies tout the fact that such people can benefit by seeking early treatment. However, the companies do not discuss what happens when no treatment is available for a genetic disease. When people learn they will develop an incurable genetic disease, the effects can be shocking, according to a 2016 study conducted by researchers at Lund University in Sweden. The researchers conducted eighteen interviews over three years with a young couple after a genetic test found that the woman is a carrier of the gene that causes Huntington's disease. This disorder destroys brain cells, resulting in uncontrolled movements and diminished mental capacity. "The results show that the long-term consequences were devastating for the family," write the researchers. "This 3-year period was characterized by anxiety, repeated suicide attempts, financial difficulties and eventually divorce."[19]

Because learning the results of genetic tests can cause deep psychological distress, the researchers urge the testing companies to offer follow-up psychological counseling to their clients. Many health care organizations now take this approach. For example, the Geisinger Health System, which offers free genetic testing to clients, requires patients to meet with their doctors to receive the results. Before speaking with the patient, the doctor is required to take a thirty-minute online tutorial to review details about genetic testing and the disorder. After receiving the results, the patient is invited to meet with his or her primary-care doctor and a genetic counselor. The doctor and patient can discuss treatment and prevention options, and the counselor can arrange long-term counseling if it is required.

At-home genetic testing companies offer counseling services, but they are optional. For example, 23andMe requires clients to take an online tutorial before viewing the test results, but the company only includes a link to the National Society of Genetic Counselors to help clients find a counselor nearby. Color Genomics offers a call-in counseling service at no additional charge, but it is up to clients to make the call. "An important component of genetic testing is the interpretation of the results with a genetic counselor and those are generally not available through these third-party companies like 23andMe," says Sora Tanjasiri, a professor and chair of the health science department at California State University, Fullerton. "They'll give a print out of what they find, but it's left up to the individual to interpret what that means for them."[20] Without the proper counseling, at-home genetic tests can do more harm than good.

People who test positive for an incurable disease often experience feelings of anger, fear, and despair. Unsure of when the disease will surface, some people begin to constantly watch for symptoms. People who test positive for genetic brain disorders like Huntington's disease often worry that any lapse of memory or display of clumsiness might signal the beginning of the end for them. Over time, fear and worry can take a toll on a person's mental and physical health. This casts doubt on the value of genetic testing. "Given how stress itself can negatively affect psychological and physical health, we should be skeptical of any technology with the potential to generate anxiety that outweighs aggregate benefit,"[21] writes Daniel Munro, professor of ethics at the University of Ottawa's Graduate School of Public and International Affairs.

People who have a deadly genetic disease in their family often make important life decisions based on the belief that they too will get sick or die young. If they test negative, they can experience grief and regret over

> "Given how stress itself can negatively affect psychological and physical health, we should be skeptical of any technology with the potential to generate anxiety that outweighs aggregate benefit."[21]
>
> —Daniel Munro, professor of ethics at the University of Ottawa

False Positives in At-Home Tests Can Negatively Affect Care

In a 2018 study, researchers identified what they described as an alarmingly high rate of false positives in the raw data sent to consumers who purchase at-home genetic tests. The study found a false-positive rate of 40 percent in the tests for certain genetic mutations that are associated with high risk of disease. This poses a danger to consumers, who might experience extreme stress and seek invasive medical procedures that they do not need. Consultation with a trained genetic counselor might avoid this response, but direct-to-consumer testing does not require these consultations.

Source: Stephany Tandy-Connor, et al., "False-Positive Results Released by Direct-to-Consumer Genetic Tests Highlight the Importance of Clinical Confirmation Testing for Appropriate Patient Care," *Genetics in Medicine*, March 22, 2018. www.nature.com.

the decisions they made. For example, a French woman named Mariannick Caniou knew that her mother had Huntington's disease. Certain that she too would develop the disease, Caniou decided not to marry or have children. When a genetic test showed that she did not have the deadly gene, rather than being happy about that result, she became depressed. "Everything I had built, my life, seemed no more substantial than air,"[22] she says.

Incomplete Results

Finding out that one does not carry a disease-related gene can have other negative consequences as well. Knowing that they have a clean bill of genetic health can lull some people into a false sense of security. However, genes are only one factor in many diseases. Environmental factors and a person's lifestyle can also contribute to some diseases. People who test negative for genetic diseases sometimes make unhealthy lifestyle choices and fail to get regular checkups in the mistaken belief that they are immune from cancer and other diseases. "If I turn up negative on a risk factor for diabetes, that doesn't mean I can go eat at fast food joints every day," says Arthur Caplan, a bioethicist at New York University. Commenting on the practice of giving home genetic test kits as gifts, Caplan suggests that it would be better to "talk to your [family] about exercise, diet, climate change, pollution, wearing a seat belt or bike helmet and getting enough sleep."[23]

> "Years of repressed memories and emotions uncorked and resulted in tumultuous times that have torn my nuclear family apart."[24]
>
> —George Doe, reproductive biologist and at-home genetic testing customer

The danger of developing a false sense of security is especially acute for those using at-home genetic kits, because they only test a limited number of genes. For example, in March 2018 home genetic test provider 23andMe introduced the first over-the-counter breast cancer screening kit. The test looks for three mutations in the BRCA1 and BRCA2 genes that are commonly linked to people at higher risk for breast and ovarian cancer. The test does not look for many other cancer-related genes, including other variants of BRCA1 and BRCA2. A woman who tests negative for the genes analyzed by 23andMe might think she is safe when she is not. In fact, only one in four cases of breast cancer involve these genes.

Family Secrets

Medical conditions are not the only kind of information that creates problems and stress for genetic test consumers. These tests can reveal a wide range of family secrets, usually linked to paternity. This can include learning that a couple used a sperm donor to start a family, that a child was adopted, or that a man fathered a child outside of a marriage. Learning such information can be traumatic. For example, a reproductive biologist who calls himself George Doe took a genetic test in 2014 and learned that he had a half brother who was conceived outside his parents' marriage. Uncovering the secret devastated Doe's family. "Years of repressed memories and emotions uncorked and resulted in tumultuous times that have torn my nuclear family apart," Doe wrote. "My parents divorced. No one is talking to my dad. We're not anywhere close to being healed yet and I don't know how long it will take to put the pieces back together."[24]

Genetic testing has raced ahead of society, law, and ethics. People are not equipped to understand what a genetic test means or to cope with the emotional fallout of gaining unwanted knowledge. Until they are, genetic testing should be reserved for the medical setting, where doctors can explain results and counselors stand by to help the patients deal with what they learn.

Chapter Three

Is Genetic Testing a Threat to Privacy?

Genetic Testing Is a Threat to Privacy

- DNA samples are unique to individuals and can never be made truly anonymous.
- User agreements allow genetic testing companies to sell and share genetic data.
- The government can collect genetic information without a person's consent.

The Debate at a Glance

Genetic Testing Is Not a Threat to Privacy

- Private genetic testing companies protect the privacy of their clients.
- The NIH safeguards the privacy of genetic research participants.
- Federal laws protect the privacy of genetic data contained in medical records.
- There is no financial incentive to steal genetic data.

Genetic Testing Is a Threat to Privacy

"Genetic-testing companies cannot guarantee privacy. And many are actively selling user data to outside parties."

—Peter Pitts, president of the Center for Medicine in the Public Interest

Peter Pitts, "The Privacy Delusions of Genetic Testing," *Forbes*, February 15, 2017. www.forbes.com.

Consider these questions as you read:

1. Do you think it is possible to keep DNA databases secure? Why or why not?
2. Should genetic testing companies be able to share a person's genome with researchers or other entities as long as no personal identifying information is included? Explain your answer.
3. Should people be concerned that genetic information gathered today might be used to identify individuals at some point in the future? Why or why not?

Editor's note: The discussion that follows presents common arguments made in support of this perspective, reinforced by facts, quotes, and examples taken from various sources.

In January 2018 cold case investigator Paul Holes of the Sacramento Police Department uploaded genetic evidence from a crime scene into GEDmatch, a genetic genealogy website that allows users to compare samples of DNA against a database of roughly 1 million profiles. The DNA sample Holes uploaded came from the crime scene of a rape and murder committed thirty-seven years earlier by a serial killer called the Golden State Killer, an offender believed to be responsible for at least twelve murders and fifty rapes. Holes found ten to twenty partial DNA

41

Genetic Data Privacy Is a Concern

Many Americans are concerned about the confidentiality of genetic information, according to a national poll conducted by the Associated Press-NORC Center for Public Affairs Research. Companies that sell direct-to-consumer genetic testing services elicit the most concern. But even medical researchers and doctors are suspect when it comes to sharing genetic data.

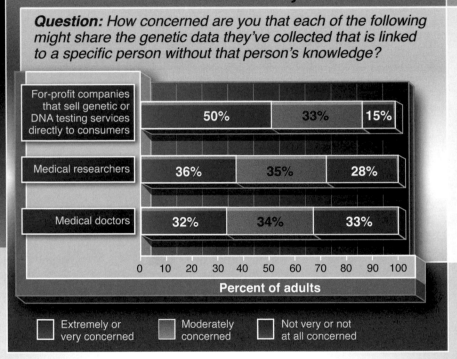

Americans Are Uneasy About the Confidentiality of Genetic Data

Question: *How concerned are you that each of the following might share the genetic data they've collected that is linked to a specific person without that person's knowledge?*

	Extremely or very concerned	Moderately concerned	Not very or not at all concerned
For-profit companies that sell genetic or DNA testing services directly to consumers	50%	33%	15%
Medical researchers	36%	35%	28%
Medical doctors	32%	34%	33%

Percent of adults

Source: Emily Swanson et al., "Genetic Testing: Ancestry Interest, but Privacy Concerns," Associated Press, July 27, 2018. https://reports.norc.org.

matches in the database, coming from distant cousins of the killer. Holes used public records, obituaries, newspaper clippings, and other data to find a common ancestor of the offender and the cousins—their great-great-great grandparents from the early 1800s. Using the website Ancestry.com, Holes then built family trees from the common ancestors back to the present, looking for a living descendant who fit the age and location of the Golden State Killer.

The detective work led to several people, including Joseph James DeAngelo, a former police officer who had been fired from his job after being caught shoplifting. Officers followed DeAngelo for a week and obtained some of his DNA from the handle of his car while he shopped. It was a perfect match to the Golden State Killer's DNA. To be doubly sure, officers obtained a second DNA sample from a used tissue in DeAngelo's trash. It was another match. They arrested DeAngelo on April 24, 2018. He has been charged with twelve counts of murder in four California counties.

The public rightly applauds Holes and all of the police who brought DeAngelo to justice, but the case raises genetic privacy issues as well. The techniques used on DeAngelo can be used to identify anyone who has ever provided a genetic sample to a genealogy website, research laboratory, or law enforcement official or even had blood or tissue taken for medical testing. "Even the people who consent by uploading their DNA often don't imagine the ways their information will be used," says Erin Murphy, a law professor at New York University. "They aren't really thinking through the implications of creating this treasure trove of data that can be mined."[25]

A Unique Marker

A person does not have to be a criminal to want to remain unknown. Sperm donors, mothers who have left a newborn with a hospital or police under "safe haven" laws, or parents who put a child up for adoption might want and expect privacy for their decisions. All people have a right to privacy, and they are not required to explain why. Yet many are at risk of being identified through their DNA, even if they have not given consent for it to be collected.

The problem is that each person's DNA is unique to him or her (unless the person is an identical twin). "A DNA sample therefore can never be made truly anonymized,"[26] states the National Human Genome Research Institute. A study by Yaniv Erlich, a geneticist at the Whitehead Institute for Biomedical Research in Cambridge, Massachusetts, proves the point. Erlich's team learned the identities of five out of ten men who had anonymously donated their genomes to scientific studies.

The researchers essentially used the same techniques as the detective in the DeAngelo case. They uploaded the anonymous genomes to genealogy websites, found partial matches with identified users, and then built family trees that included the anonymous donors. They then used online information from websites such as PeopleFinders or USA People Search to identify the donors. "The issue is the current status of privacy," says Erlich. "We need to be respectful to participants, to tell them the truth: that someone can identify you."[27]

Genomes for Sale

Human genomes are a valuable commodity. Pharmaceutical companies and medical researchers need large samplings of genomic data to conduct their research, and they are willing to pay for it. For example, in 2015 biotech company Genentech paid 23andMe $10 million for the rights to sequence the entire genomes of three thousand 23andMe customers who have a higher risk for developing Parkinson's disease, a genetic disorder in which motor nerves in the brain deteriorate. The buyers of such data often share it with university laboratories and other entities so they can perform additional research to independently verify (or refute) the company's research results.

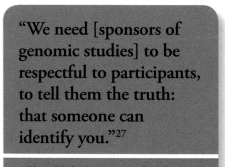

"We need [sponsors of genomic studies] to be respectful to participants, to tell them the truth: that someone can identify you."[27]

—Yaniv Erlich, a geneticist at the Whitehead Institute for Biomedical Research

Genetic testing firms have privacy policies that prevent them from sharing genetic data without the permission of their clients. However, these policies are normally explained in the companies' user agreements. User agreements for all sorts of tech-related services are notoriously difficult to understand. Clients who accept the user agreement may be unwittingly giving permission for the company to share their genetic information with others. "When was the last time any of us read through a user agreement and understood it?" asks Deborah C. Peel, founder and president of Patient Privacy Rights, a nonprofit civil rights organization. "'User agreements' that no reasonable person can understand should be litigated as fraudulent contracts."[28]

Even when people knowingly give consent, they might not realize how that decision could affect other family members. Just as detectives used genetic information from a distant relative to track down DeAngelo, someone could use a person's genetic information to identify relatives both now and at some future date. "Even if [users are] content with making that trade-off with their personal data, they're also making that trade-off with their extended family, their children, their children's children," says Erin Murphy. "And they're not just making it for 2018, but for 2020 and 2040, when data from the genome could be used in all sorts of different ways."[29]

Public Genetic Databases

Private companies are not the only collectors of genetic information and DNA samples. Various governmental agencies collect the information as well, often without consent. For example, many states require hospitals to take blood samples from newborn infants to identify children born with serious diseases, including hypothyroidism (underactivity of the thyroid gland); phenylketonuria (PKU), a disease that can lead to brain damage; and sickle-cell anemia, in which cells can become stuck in blood vessels. Parents in Texas objected to the sharing of these samples for research, and they brought a lawsuit against the state to stop it. The lawsuit succeeded, and the state was forced to destroy 5 million blood samples. As a result of this controversy, Congress passed the Newborn Screening Saves Lives Reauthorization Act, which permits the collection of blood samples from newborns but requires parental consent for their use in research. However, this law applies only to blood samples collected after March 18, 2015. DNA collected before that date can still be used; that amounts to millions of people who lost control of their most personal information at birth.

Genetic information is routinely captured, catalogued, and stored by law enforcement—even when people are not charged with crimes. In a 2013 case known as *Maryland v. King*, the US Supreme Court held that law enforcement officers may collect DNA samples from suspects who have been arrested for a crime. That DNA remains on file even if charges are later dropped. The five-justice majority reasoned that the collection of DNA is similar to the fingerprinting and photographing of arrestees and does not violate a person's Fourth Amendment protections against unreasonable search and seizure. The four dissenting justices found this troubling. Justice Antonin Scalia wrote for the minority, "Make no mistake about it: As an entirely predictable consequence of today's decision, your DNA can be taken and entered into a national DNA database if you are ever arrested, rightly or wrongly, and for whatever reason."[30] Scalia was right. The FBI's National DNA Index System (NDIS) now includes not only 13 million offender profiles but also more than 3 million arrestee profiles.

> "Make no mistake about it . . . your DNA can be taken and entered into a national DNA database if you are ever arrested, rightly or wrongly, and for whatever reason."[30]
>
> —Justice Antonin Scalia of the US Supreme Court

A person's genome never changes, and once it is sequenced, it will live on forever in the databases of the companies and laboratories that obtain it. Congress, genetic testing firms, and medical laboratories can promise privacy, but that is not a promise anyone can keep.

Genetic Testing Is Not a Threat to Privacy

"Privacy and your ownership and control of your genome is the most important—it's the foundation of this company."

—Anne Wojcicki, chief executive officer of 23andMe, a genetic testing firm

Quoted in Eric Johnson, "Is It Safe to Give Your Genetic Data to 23andMe?," Recode, September 22, 2017. www.recode.net.

Consider these questions as you read:

1. Do you believe that laws and company policies offer enough protection to people who undergo genetic testing? Why or why not?
2. Would privacy concerns prevent you from donating your genetic information for research, even if it might help save lives? Explain your answer.
3. Do you believe that concerns about the theft of genetic information are exaggerated? Why or why not?

Editor's note: The discussion that follows presents common arguments made in support of this perspective, reinforced by facts, quotes, and examples taken from various sources.

Privacy advocates are raising questions about genetic profiles being kept in various databases, including those maintained by at-home genetic testing companies, research laboratories, health care providers, and law enforcement agencies. These concerns are overstated. Genetic testing companies have tightened their privacy policies, and Congress has passed laws that make the unauthorized sharing and use of genetic data a crime. Most fundamentally, a person's genetic code is not a key that unlocks information that would be particularly valuable to anyone outside of a medical laboratory.

Privacy Is a Corporate Priority

Millions of people have entrusted their genetic information to private genetic testing companies like Ancestry.com and 23andMe. So far there has not been any sign that their trust has been misplaced. Private firms go to great lengths to protect the privacy of their clients. Most importantly, they do not make a client's genetic profile searchable by others in the database without the express permission of the user. In most cases clients must check a box to release their private information to others in the network. If a client does not do this, the information stays private. Clients also have the option of having their profile deleted from the company database once they have seen or downloaded it for their own use. It does not get much more private than that.

Clients also must give consent for their information to be shared or sold to others for research purposes. No consent, no sharing. Even if a client agrees to share the genetic profile, the company first removes all personal identification, including the client's name and address—a process known as deidentification. A 2013 study at the Massachusetts Institute of Technology showed that anonymous genetic information could be reidentified, but that study started with not only the genetic profiles but the donors' ages and the states where they lived. Without that additional information, reidentifying a DNA sample or genetic profile would be extremely difficult.

> "Under certain circumstances, personal information may be subject to disclosure pursuant to judicial or other government subpoenas. . . . We use all practical legal and administrative resources to resist such requests."[31]
>
> —Privacy policy of 23andMe

Some private genetic testing firms care so much about client privacy that they have stated that they will resist sharing genetic information with the government, including law enforcement. In its privacy statement, 23andMe states, "Under certain circumstances, personal information may be subject to disclosure pursuant to judicial or other government subpoenas, warrants or orders, or in coordination with regulatory authorities. However, we use all practical legal and administrative resources to resist such requests."[31]

Research Security

Private companies are not the only entities that have genetic information and samples. The NIH has several databases containing genetic information collected from donors. The agency recently tightened its Genomic Data Sharing Policy. A scientist seeking access to the genetic data in one of the NIH databases must request permission from the committees that oversee data access, outlining exactly how the data will be used. The committees review the proposed research to ensure that it is legitimate and the genetic information will be protected. Only genetic researchers affiliated with reputable institutions can apply to see such data or obtain DNA samples. The notion that a bad actor could pass through the review process and obtain the genetic data is far-fetched.

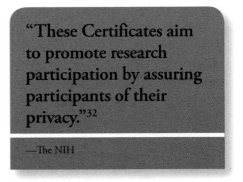

"These Certificates aim to promote research participation by assuring participants of their privacy."[32]

—The NIH

To further protect genetic information, the NIH issues Certificates of Confidentiality to researchers who are using the data and samples. These certificates ensure that researchers and their institutions cannot be forced to give up identifying information about DNA samples in any civil, criminal, or other court proceeding at federal, state, and local levels. "These Certificates aim to promote research participation by assuring participants of their privacy,"[32] states the NIH.

Genetic Security Laws

Congress has also taken action to protect the privacy of genetic data in three areas: newborn screening, medical records, and insurance. Before 2014 genetic researchers could gain access to the DNA of newborns whose blood samples were collected as part of public health programs to screen for diseases like PKU, hypothyroidism, and sickle-cell anemia. However, in 2014 Congress passed the Newborn Screening Saves Lives Reauthorization Act. This law requires parental consent for the use of infant blood samples in genetic research. Without such consent, such samples are off limits to genetic researchers.

Americans More Confident About Genetic Testing Privacy

Surveys conducted by National Public Radio and Truven Health Analytics in 2016 and 2017 found that Americans have growing confidence in the privacy of their genetic testing information. The poll found that 47.2 percent of respondents had privacy concerns in 2017, compared to 59.1 percent just a year earlier. When broken out by age, education, and income, nearly all groups expressed less concern in 2017 than in 2016.

Question: *Do you have any privacy concerns regarding your or your family member's genetic information and how it could be used by others?*

Have privacy concerns	2017	2016
Age		
<35	53.9%	70%
35–64	45.1%	49.9%
65+	23%	43.1%
Education		
HS or Less	40%	69.7%
Some College/Associate	36.3%	45%
College+	51.6%	61.4%

Source: The Truven Health Analytics-NPR Health Poll, "Genetic Testing," March 2018, p. 12. https://truvenhealth.com.

Blood and tissue samples collected at hospitals and doctors' offices during medical procedures are also a source of genetic information. However, the privacy of medical records is governed by a federal law known as the Health Insurance Portability and Accountability Act (HIPAA). In 2013 the HIPAA Privacy Rule was revised to cover genetic information. As a result, health care providers and insurance companies may not use or disclose identified genetic information for the purpose of making decisions about a person's insurability or insurance rates.

Regardless of how genetic information is obtained or where it is stored, its use is further governed by the Genetic Information and Non-discrimination Act of 2008. This federal law protects Americans against employment and insurance discrimination based on their genetic information. Anyone who violates the law not only could face federal criminal charges but also could be liable for damages in civil court.

Federal law also ensures that the FBI's NDIS is secure. The database contains the DNA profiles of some 16 million convicts and arrestees. However, the NDIS contains no names or other personal identifiers associated with the DNA profiles. The information about the person behind the DNA profile is stored at the state level. Even if unauthorized persons gained access to the FBI database, they would not be able to match DNA profiles to the people behind them. In addition, the NDIS only identifies repeated sections of the DNA strand, known as short tandem repeats. These are not genes. They reveal little about the appearance or medical conditions of a person. The FBI also allows the DNA profiles to be used for research, but only when all identifiers have been removed from the file. The computers containing the system's software are located in a physically secure space, and access is given only to individuals approved by the FBI. This data is secure.

A Question of Worth

Perhaps the biggest deterrent to stealing genetic information is that it has no financial value. Nevertheless, privacy advocates and journalists have tried mightily to suggest otherwise. "Your genes don't determine everything about who you are, but they do contain revealing information about your health, relationships, personality, and family history that, like a social security number, could be easily abused,"[33] writes Kristen V. Brown for the tech website Gizmodo. The comparison to a Social Security number sounds scary, but the analogy does not hold up. A criminal with another person's Social Security number can use it to steal that person's identity and gain access to credit histories, bank and credit card accounts, and other financial information. By contrast, a criminal with another person's genome cannot use it to steal an identity or access any financial information. The thief could learn something about the person's health, but only if the thief happens to be a geneticist on the side. A genome will not provide information about a person's relationships or personality. If it is plugged into a genealogic website, it could reveal something about family history, but it is hard to see how a data thief could profit by such information. Without a financial incentive, there is no reason for anyone to obtain a person's genetic information.

Genetic information is protected by state and federal law, governmental policies, and the privacy policies for genetic testing firms. The only entities that would financially benefit from gaining access to genetic data—insurance companies and employers—are forbidden from using it for financial gain. Genetic testing simply does not threaten personal privacy.

Chapter Four

Are Genetically Modified Foods Safe?

Genetically Modified Foods Are Not Safe

- Biological engineers introduce dangerous allergens into foods to combat pests.
- Genetically modified organisms can crossbreed or cross-pollinate with natural organisms, contaminating the food supply and endangering the environment.
- The long-term effects of genetically modified foods are not known.

The Debate at a Glance

Genetically Modified Foods Are Safe

- Genetically modified foods are just a more advanced method of crossbreeding.
- Genetically modified foods reduce the need for pesticides that pollute the environment.
- No credible scientific study has found genetically modified foods to be harmful.

Genetically Modified Foods Are Not Safe

"Introducing foreign genetic materials has unpredictable consequences, and once the mutant genes are out of the bag, there's no going back."

—Katerina Konecna, a member of the European Parliament representing the Czech Republic

Quoted in Debating Europe, "Should GMOs Be Banned Across Europe?," March 15, 2018. www.debatingeurope.eu.

Consider these questions as you read:

1. Would you consider eating salmon that has been modified with a gene from another species of salmon? Why or why not?
2. Why are genetically modified foods described as posing a threat to the environment, and can these threats be controlled? Explain.
3. Do you think genetically modified foods should be banned, even if some people are willing to eat them? Explain your answer.

Editor's note: The discussion that follows presents common arguments made in support of this perspective, reinforced by facts, quotes, and examples taken from various sources.

The first sign that something bad was happening to the food supply came in 2000, when a woman named Grace Booth went into allergic shock after eating three tacos made with Taco Bell taco shells. These were not ordinary taco shells. They had been made with corn that contained a pest-repelling gene that had been inserted into its genome by genetic engineers. Following Booth's ordeal, Kraft Foods, which distributed the Taco Bell shells, pulled the contaminated food item from supermarket shelves. It was the first-ever product recall of a food because of its genetically engineered ingredients.

Many US Consumers Doubt Safety of Genetically Modified Foods

Many US consumers have concerns about the safety of genetically modified foods, according to a 2018 survey by the International Food Information Council Foundation. Seventy-two percent of survey respondents said they were concerned or very concerned about the effects of GM foods on human health. The effects of GM foods on the environment, on animals, and on farming also raised concerns. Additionally, 51 percent of respondents said they would have concerns about feeding their children GM foods.

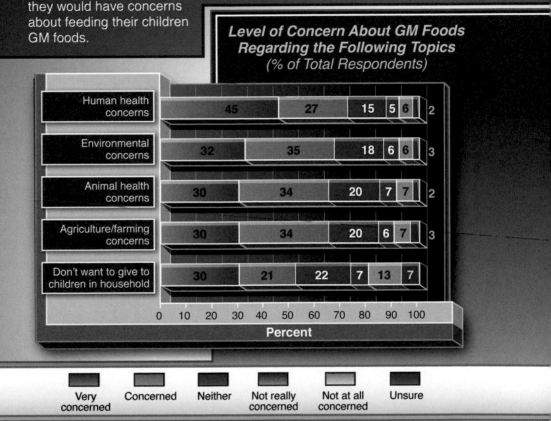

Level of Concern About GM Foods Regarding the Following Topics
(% of Total Respondents)

	Very concerned	Concerned	Neither	Not really concerned	Not at all concerned	Unsure
Human health concerns	45	27	15	5	6	2
Environmental concerns	32	35	18	6	6	3
Animal health concerns	30	34	20	7	7	2
Agriculture/farming concerns	30	34	20	6	7	3
Don't want to give to children in household	30	21	22	7	13	7

Percent

Source: *IFIC Foundation Survey*, International Food Information Council Foundation, June 2018. www.foodinsight.org.

Scientists edit the genomes of edible plants and animals to make them more resistant to pests and disease in the hopes of increasing agricultural yields and profits. A plant or animal that has had its genome altered is known as a genetically modified organism, or GMO. The genetic modification can include removing, or knocking out, a specific gene without replacing it. It can also include inserting a gene from one species into the genome of another species, using a technique known as recombinant DNA. The modified organism is known as a transgenic organism. The US Environmental Protection Agency and the FDA have approved some GMOs, including transgenic organisms, for consumption by human beings. Other GMOs have been approved for consumption by animals, many of which are later consumed by human beings. These are known as genetically modified (GM) foods—and they are contributing to the unexplained rise in allergies seen in recent decades.

Physical Reactions to GM Corn

An investigation into the Taco Bell taco shells revealed that the corn used to make them was contaminated with Starlink corn, a GMO that had been approved for animal feed but not for human consumption. Starlink and other GM corns contain genes from a common soil bacterium known as *Bacillus thuringiensis* (Bt). The Bt gene expresses a protein that is highly toxic to the European corn borer, a corn-eating caterpillar. The FDA did not approve Starlink corn for human consumption, because it was concerned that the toxic protein might be difficult to digest and might cause an allergic reaction in people. Grace Booth's reaction to the taco shells suggests the FDA was right.

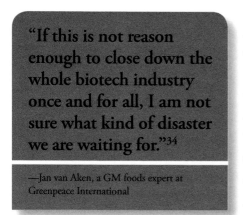

"If this is not reason enough to close down the whole biotech industry once and for all, I am not sure what kind of disaster we are waiting for."[34]

—Jan van Aken, a GM foods expert at Greenpeace International

The FDA has found that another GM corn that contains Bt genes, MON810, is safe for human consumption. It is used in corn oil, corn syrup, and many other foods in the United States. The governments of six countries in Europe—Austria, France, Germany, Greece, Hungary, and Luxembourg— disagree with the FDA's finding. They have banned foods made with MON810 on the grounds that it poses a risk to human health.

These countries were influenced by various research studies, including one led by Jürgen Zentek, a professor of veterinary medicine at the University of Vienna. Zentek's team found that mice that were fed MON810 were less fertile than those fed conventional corn. "Genetically Engineered food appears to be acting as a birth control agent, potentially leading to infertility," said Jan van Aken, a GM foods expert at Greenpeace International. "If this is not reason enough to close down the whole biotech industry once and for all, I am not sure what kind of disaster we are waiting for."[34]

Genetically Engineered Salmon

In addition to GM corn, the FDA has approved GM apples, papaya, summer squash, sugar beets, alfalfa, canola, and potatoes for human consumption. In 2016 it also approved the first GM animal for human consumption: a genetically engineered Atlantic salmon produced by a food company named AquaBounty Technologies. The company's genetic engineers added a gene from a different species of salmon, the Pacific Chinook salmon, to the Atlantic salmon genome. The Pacific Chinook salmon gene produces a hormone that allows the Atlantic salmon to grow all year, instead of only during the warmer months, as it does in nature. By growing year round, these transgenic salmon reach a marketable weight in just eighteen months, rather than the thirty months it normally takes. This makes the fish grown in a fish farm much more profitable than natural fish.

But the growth hormone concerns some experts. "These fish are engineered to have way more growth hormones than normal," says Jaydee Hanson, a policy analyst at the Center for Food Safety, an advocacy group that is suing the FDA over its approval of the GM salmon for consumption in the United States. "We know, from the growth hormones that are put in beef, that they can create a hormone called IGF,"[35] Hanson explains. A 2015 study by researchers at the University of North Carolina–Chapel Hill found that high levels of IGF play an important role in the development and progression of many cancers.

Experts are also concerned about possible allergens in the AquaBounty GM salmon. There have been no allergy studies on people who have eaten the fish. The tests only looked at the amount of known allergens in the fish, and the tests—which involved just six fish—were inconclusive. "Because FDA's assessment is inadequate, we are particularly concerned that this salmon may pose an increased risk of severe, even life-threatening allergic reactions to sensitive individuals,"[36] writes Michael Hansen, a senior scientist with Consumers Union, a consumer advocacy group.

Environmental Concerns

In addition to posing a health risk, GM foods also threaten to contaminate the environment through cross-pollination and crossbreeding. This in turn poses a risk to the food supply. An incident of this sort has already occurred with the Starlink corn that contaminated the Taco Bell taco shells. Although this corn was intended for use only as animal feed and not as food for humans, pollen from the GM corn plants became airborne and cross-pollinated corn crops being grown for human consumption. When the cross-pollinated corn matured, it was harvested and used in the taco shells that made Grace Booth ill.

Environmentalists fear the same—or worse—could happen if Aqua-Bounty's "frankenfish" escaped from the fish ponds where they are being grown. Dune Lankard, a salmon fisher and spokesperson for the Center for Biological Diversity, points out that the growth gene that makes the GM salmon more profitable also gives them an advantage in the wild. "Once they escape, you can't put these transgenic fish back in the bag," says Lankard.

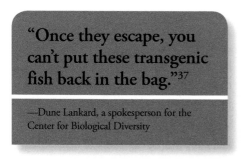

"Once they escape, you can't put these transgenic fish back in the bag."[37]

—Dune Lankard, a spokesperson for the Center for Biological Diversity

"They're manufactured to outgrow wild salmon, and if they cross-breed, it could have irreversible impacts on the natural world."[37] The larger, faster-growing fish could outcompete the natural salmon, driving them to extinction.

The environmental concern forms a second prong of the Center for Food Safety's lawsuit. It charges that the FDA made its decision without fully considering the environmental risks. "This case is about protecting our fisheries and ocean ecosystems from the foreseeable harms of the first-ever [genetically engineered] fish, harms FDA refused to even consider, let alone prevent,"[38] says George Kimbrell, an attorney for the Center for Food Safety.

An Unknown Risk

One of the problems with GM foods is that the long-term effects of consuming them could be harmful. For example, Jürgen Zentek's team found that infertility increased with each successive litter because the mice had been feeding on the GM corn longer. No one knows what the long-term effects of ingesting the proteins that are toxic to pests like the European corn borer will be. It is possible that toxins could accumulate in fat tissue or organs over many years before they begin to cause harm. Some scientists worry that bacteria in the human gut might absorb DNA from GMOs and become altered in a natural process known as horizontal gene transfer. These altered bacteria could prove harmful to humans.

It is possible that by the time the negative effects of "frankenfoods" begin to show up in humans, millions of people will have already consumed them, possibly for decades. By then it will be too late to reverse the effects. With natural alternatives to GM foods all around us, it is time to ban these genetic monsters.

Genetically Modified Foods Are Safe

"In the decades since the first genetically modified foods reached the market, no adverse health effects among consumers have been found. This is not to say there are none, but as hard as opponents of the technology have looked, none have yet been definitely identified."

—Jane E. Brody, author on science and nutrition topics

Jane E. Brody, "Are G.M.O. Foods Safe?," *New York Times*, April 23, 2018. www.nytimes.com.

Consider these questions as you read:

1. Do you believe that all tools available to humanity, including GM foods, should be used to reduce global hunger? Why or why not?
2. Do you think reducing pesticide pollution is a good reason to use GM foods? Explain.
3. What can be done to ensure that government and public policies concerning GM foods are guided by good information?

Editor's note: The discussion that follows presents common arguments made in support of this perspective, reinforced by facts, quotes, and examples taken from various sources.

Every day, 700 million people worldwide fail to get enough to eat, and by 2030 the world will have another 1 billion people to feed. Even with advances in agricultural methods and technology, the Food and Agriculture Organization of the United Nations estimates that as much as 40 percent of the world's crops are lost to insects, weeds, and plant diseases each year. If there is a safe and efficient way to make sure that people the world over have enough food to eat, humanity has a moral obligation to do this. And as it happens, there is. GM foods are a safe and efficient way to increase crop yields. "GM technology has the potential to produce more food with less pollution,"[39] states Qiang Wang, professor at the Xinjiang Institute of Ecology and Geography of the Chinese Academy of Sciences in Urumqi, China.

Targeted Changes

Most people consider genetically modifying foods to be a very recent development, but people have been engineering foods by crossbreeding different strains or subspecies of plants and animals for centuries. The goal then, as now, was to create tastier, hardier, more resilient crops. Traditional crossbreeding involves large, imprecise exchanges of genetic material. Over time, through this process, farmers developed tastier, hardier, more resilient strains of apples, oranges, corn, and other crops. Genetic engineering accomplishes the same basic goals but is more precise and thus can be done on a much larger scale. It usually targets a specific gene that is known to produce a desirable quality. For example, the FDA has recently approved GM apples that do not turn brown when eaten or sliced (a benefit to consumers) and GM potatoes that do not bruise (a benefit to stores that sell produce).

One of the best examples of targeted gene editing involves GM corn. Decades ago scientists learned that the common soil bacteria Bt expresses a protein, known as Cry1F, that is deadly to caterpillars, including the European corn borer. This pest is nicknamed the "billion dollar bug" because it causes about $1 billion in crop damage each year in the United States alone. Cry1F is not toxic to adult insects or to other species. This is because the protein can only bind to certain receptors on cells, just as a certain key will only open a certain lock. Caterpillars have these receptors in their guts, but other insects do not. Neither do birds, reptiles, or mammals, including livestock and human beings. Geneticists practicing recombinant DNA inserted the Bt genes into the corn genome so the plants could produce

> "GM technology has the potential to produce more food with less pollution."[39]
>
> —Qiang Wang, professor at the Xinjiang Institute of Ecology and Geography of the Chinese Academy of Sciences in Urumqi, China

Research Does Not Find Links Between Genetically Modified Foods and Diseases

Research does not support assertions of a link between consumption of genetically modified foods and various diseases. The incidence of various types of cancer in US women, for instance, shows no obvious change over several decades. If GM foods were causing a substantial number of cancers, researchers say, the incidence would be higher after 1996, when GM foods (specifically, soybeans and corn) were first grown in the United States. The researchers also noted a lack of evidence for supposed relationships between GM foods and kidney disease, type 2 diabetes, obesity, and food allergies.

Trends in Cancer Incidence in Women in the United States

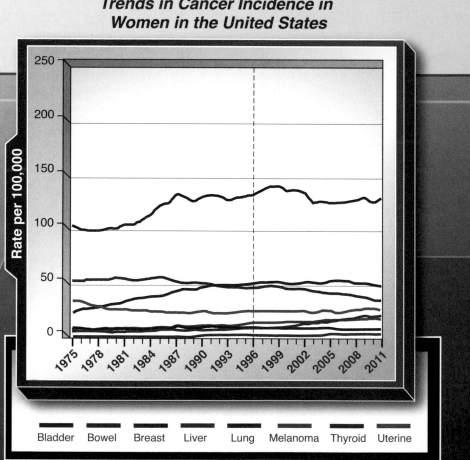

Note: Dashed line at 1996 indicates year GM soybeans and corn were first grown in the United States.

Source: "Genetically Engineered Crops: Experiences and Prospects." National Academies of Sciences, Engineering, and Medicine, 2016. www.nap.edu.

the pest-repelling proteins. A caterpillar that bites into the GM corn stops eating instantly and dies within a matter of hours. Now, more than 80 percent of all corn grown in the United States includes the Bt genes.

Using genetics to stop the European corn borer also prevents the GM corn from contracting diseases. When the corn borer feeds on non-GM corn, it leaves chewed areas open to the atmosphere, where airborne fungus and bacteria can land and infect the corn. Some of these diseases produce toxic and cancer-causing compounds in the plant. By stopping the corn borer before damage is done, GM corn is able to resist disease as well, making it safer for both animals and people to eat. A February 2018 study by researchers in Pisa, Italy, found that GM corn contains lower amounts of toxins produced by fungi than natural corn does.

Benefiting the Environment

Genetic engineering has also reduced the need for plants to be sprayed with pesticides. Equipped with the Bt gene, GM corn is able to make its own, targeted pesticide. According to the US Department of Agriculture (USDA), farmers planting GM corn use 36 percent less pesticide than those using non-GM corn. Overall, the amount of pesticide used per acre of corn decreased by 99 percent between 1995 and 2010.

Part of the reason less pesticide is being used is that there are fewer damaging pests to kill; the GM corn is wiping out the corn borer before it has time to mature and lay eggs. Fewer eggs means fewer corn borers. The cycle repeats itself with each generation until the number of pests is negligible. Pesticides are highly toxic to people and to animals. By reducing the amount of pesticide being sprayed, GM crops are decreasing the amount of pesticide farmers are exposed to, increasing their safety. In addition, GM crops reduce the amount of pesticide in the soil and surface water, which reduces pollution of the environment and increases the safety of wildlife.

Anti-GM Hysteria

Despite their obvious advantages, GM foods are not endorsed by everyone. In fact, six European countries have banned their cultivation. The European officials who made the anti-GMO decisions relied on research that has been shown to be flawed. The most sensational of these studies was conducted by researchers led by French molecular biologist Gilles-Éric Séralini of the University of Caen. Their 2012 study found that rats fed for two years with GM corn developed many more tumors and died earlier than rats on normal diets. At a press conference, Séralini showed pictures of rats with large tumors. Not surprisingly, the effects were immediate. "Yes, GMOs are poisons,"[40] shouted the front cover of *Le Nouvel Observateur*, a French weekly newsmagazine. "News of the horrifying findings is spreading fast, with even the mainstream media in shock over the photos of rats with multiple grotesque tumors; tumors so large the rats even had difficulty breathing in some cases,"[41] said the website Food Matters. Based on Séralini's study, Russia stopped importing GM corn, and Kenya banned all GM crops.

> "The results showed that the two GM [corn] varieties tested did not trigger any negative effects in the trial animals."[42]
>
> —GMO Risk Assessment and Communication of Evidence, a project of the European Commission

Scientists immediately questioned Séralini's study. The European Food Safety Authority in Parma, Italy, stated that the paper's conclusions were not supported by the data presented. The initial doubts about Séralini's research have since been confirmed. In 2018 two studies funded by the European Union and one funded by France refuted Séralini's conclusions. Researchers in the GMO Risk Assessment and Communication of Evidence study conducted two ninety-day feeding trials on rats using two different varieties of GM corn. "The results showed that the two GM [corn] varieties tested did not trigger any negative effects in the trial animals,"[42] states the report. The GM Plant Two Year Safety Testing report agreed. After a two-year test feeding rats with a different type of GM corn, the researchers came to a similar conclusion. They found no negative effects.

The anti-GM food hysteria has not died down in Europe. In 2017 a majority of European Union countries voted against allowing two new GM crops, Pioneer's 1507 and Syngenta's Bt11, to be grown in Europe. Then, in July 2018, the European Union's highest court ruled that crops with genomes edited using CRISPR-Cas9 are GMOs, and therefore must comply with extremely tight regulations. "I don't know why they are doing that," says Jennifer Kuzma, a professor of genetic engineering policy at North Carolina State University. "I was thinking, 'Do they have the right science advice?'"[43]

Part of the reason for European opposition to GM foods is that the people making policy decisions are elected officials, and many are unwilling to take positions that might get them voted out of office. Polls consistently show that about 70 percent of the European public believes GM foods are unsafe. The fears ignited by the research of Séralini and others have not died down despite "hundreds of millions of genetic experiments involving every type of organism on earth and people eating billions of meals without a problem,"[44] says Robert Goldberg, a molecular biologist at the University of California, Los Angeles.

GM crops produce greater crop yields, reduce pollution, and can help alleviate hunger. The FDA, USDA, American Medical Association, National Academy of Sciences, and World Health Organization have all concluded that they are safe for consumption. People eat GM foods every day with no evidence of harm. They are an important part of our future.

Overview: Rearranging the Building Blocks of Life

1. Quoted in Jocelyn Kaiser, "Gene Therapy's New Hope: A Neuron-Targeting Virus Is Saving Infant Lives," *Science*, November 1, 2017. www.sciencemag.org.
2. Quoted in Kaiser, "Gene Therapy's New Hope."
3. Francis S. Collins, "Contemplating the End of the Beginning," *Genome Research*, May 2001. https://genome.cshlp.org.
4. Quoted in US Food and Drug Administration, "FDA Approves Novel Gene Therapy to Treat Patients with a Rare Form of Inherited Vision Loss," December 19, 2017. www.fda.gov.
5. National Institutes of Health, "What Are Genome Editing and CRISPR-Cas9?," Genetics Home Reference, July 17, 2018. https://ghr.nlm.nih.gov.

Chapter One: Is Genetic Engineering Ethical?

6. Quoted in David Cyranoski and Sara Reardon, "Chinese Scientists Genetically Modify Human Embryos," *Nature*, April 22, 2015. www.nature.com.
7. Francis S. Collins, "Experts Debate: Are We Playing with Fire When We Edit Human Genes?," STAT, November 17, 2015. www.statnews.com.
8. Quoted in Amy Harmon, "The Problem with an Almost-Perfect Genetic World," *New York Times*, November 20, 2005. www.nytimes.com.
9. Marcy Darnovsky, "Pro and Con: Should Gene Editing Be Performed on Human Embryos?," *National Geographic*, August 2016. www.nationalgeographic.com.
10. Quoted in Ian Sample, "Editing Embryo DNA Is an Exciting Landmark, but in Reality Will Benefit Few," *Guardian* (Manchester), August 4, 2017. www.theguardian.com.
11. Quoted in David Cyranoski, "Ethics of Embryo Editing Divides Scientists," *Nature*, March 18, 2015. www.nature.com.
12. Quoted in Akshat Rathi, "A Highly Successful Attempt at Genetic Editing of Human Embryos Has Opened the Door to Eradicating Inherited Diseases," Quartz, August 2, 2017. https://qz.com.

Chapter Two: Is Genetic Testing Beneficial?

13. Quoted in Anne Wojcicki, "A Major Milestone in Consumer Health Empowerment," *23andMeBlog*, March 6, 2018. https://blog.23andme.com.

14. Sara Faye Green, "I Took a Home Genetic Test and Got Scary Results," *Women's Health*, November 8, 2017. www.womenshealthmag.com.

15. Jyoti Patel, "Genetic Testing and Cancer—an Introduction to Personalized Medicine," Cancer.Net, April 11, 2018. www.cancer.net.

16. Quoted in National Institutes of Health, "Personalized Medicine," NIH News in Health, December 2013. https://newsinhealth.nih.gov.

17. Quoted in Anna Medaris Miller, "Should You Take a Genetic Test to Find the Best Diet for You?," *U.S. News & World Report*, January 16, 2018. https://health.usnews.com.

18. Quoted in Michelle Andrews, "What If Your Doctor Offered Genetic Testing as a Way to Keep You Healthy?," *Washington Post*, May 28, 2018. www.washingtonpost.com.

19. Petra Lilja Andersson et al., "Ethical Aspects of a Predictive Test for Huntington's Disease," *Nursing Ethics*, August 2016. www.ncbi.nlm.nih.gov.

20. Quoted in Tricia Lasha, "At-Home Genetic Tests Can Give Misleading Results," *Daily Titan* (California State University, Fullerton), March 19, 2018. https://dailytitan.com.

21. Daniel Munro, "The Dangers of Mail-In Genetic Testing," *Maclean's*, June 5, 2017. www.macleans.ca.

22. Quoted in Laura Spinney, "We Don't Want to Know What Will Kill Us," *Slate*, September 29, 2017. www.slate.com.

23. Quoted in Natalie Rahhal, "'Genetics Have a Dark Side': Trend of Gifting DNA Tests Might Be More of a Curse than a Joy This Christmas, Ethicist Warns," *Daily Mail* (London), December 18, 2017. www.dailymail.co.uk.

24. George Doe, "With Genetic Testing, I Gave My Parents the Gift of Divorce," Vox, September 9, 2014. www.vox.com.

Chapter Three: Is Genetic Testing a Threat to Privacy?

25. Quoted in Justin Jouvenal et al., "Data on a Genealogy Site Led Police to the 'Golden State Killer' Suspect. Now Others Worry About a 'Treasure Trove of Data,'" *Washington Post*, April 27, 2018. www.washingtonpost.com.

26. National Human Genome Research Institute, "Privacy in Genomics," April 21, 2015. www.genome.gov.

27. Quoted in Kevin Jiang, "Anonymity Not Guaranteed: Identity of Personal Genomic DNA Revealed by Web Search," *Spoonful of Medicine* (blog), *Nature Medicine*, January 17, 2013. http://blogs.nature.com.

28. Deborah C. Peel, "The Hidden Danger of Do-It-Yourself Genetic Tests," *Newsweek*, March 7, 2017. www.newsweek.com.

29. Quoted in Jouvenal et al., "Data on a Genealogy Site Led Police to the 'Golden State Killer' Suspect. Now Others Worry About a 'Treasure Trove of Data.'"

30. Quoted in Justia, "Maryland v. King, 569 U.S. 435 (2013)." https://supreme.justia.com.

31. Quoted in Eric Rosenbaum, "5 Biggest Risks of Sharing Your DNA with Consumer Genetic-Testing Companies," CNBC, June 16, 2018. www.cnbc.com.

32. National Human Genome Research Institute, "Privacy in Genomics."

33. Kristen V. Brown, "What DNA Testing Companies' Terrifying Privacy Policies Actually Mean," Gizmodo, October 18, 2017. https://gizmodo.com.

Chapter Four: Are Genetically Modified Foods Safe?

34. Quoted in Sean Poulter, "Why Eating GM Food Could Lower Your Fertility," *Daily Mail* (London), November 12, 2008. www.dailymail.co.uk.

35. Quoted in Tamara Pearson, "Investigative Report: Are You Eating Genetically Modified Salmon? Here's How to Know," Alternative Daily, September 27, 2017. www.thealternativedaily.com.

36. Quoted in Sayer Ji, "Research Exposes New Health Risks of Genetically Modified Mosquitoes & Salmon," Collective Evolution, February 26, 2018. www.collective-evolution.com.

37. Quoted in Chris D'Angelo, "FDA Sued over Approval of Genetically Engineered Salmon," *Huffington Post*, March 31, 2016. www.huffingtonpost.com.

38. Quoted in "Lawsuit Challenges FDA's Approval of Genetically Engineered Salmon," Center for Food Safety, March 31, 2016. www.centerforfoodsafety.org.

39. Qiang Wang, "China's Scientists Must Engage the Public on GM," *Nature*, March 3, 2015. www.nature.com.

40. Quoted in *Nature*, "Poison Postures," September 25, 2012. www.nature.com.

41. Food Matters, "GMO Corn Linked to Cancer Tumors," January 7, 2013. www.foodmatters.com.

42. Quoted in Joan Conrow, "European Studies Disprove Seralini's GMO Maize Tumor Claims," Cornell Alliance for Science, June 7, 2018. https://allianceforscience.cornell.edu.

43. Quoted in Carl Zimmer, "What Is a Genetically Modified Crop? A European Ruling Sows Confusion," *New York Times*, July 27, 2018. www.nytimes.com.

44. Quoted in Jane E. Brody, "Are G.M.O. Foods Safe?," *New York Times*, April 23, 2018. www.nytimes.com.

Genetic Testing and Research Facts

At-Home Genetic Testing

- About 10 million to 15 million Americans have already taken at-home genetic tests.
- One in twenty-five American adults now have access to personal genetic data.
- By 2022 the at-home genetic testing market will grow to $340 million.
- Within ten years global sales of genetic tests are expected to hit $10 billion.
- At-home testing technology takes about 1 million measurements of a person's genome.

The Human Genome

- The human genome has 21,667 known genes, which is four times more genes than a fruit fly (4,751) but fewer than a mouse (22,723) and about the same as a worm (20,049).
- Genes make up only about 1.5 percent of the human genome.
- About 98 percent of the human genome is composed of noncoding DNA.
- More than 50 percent of the human genome is repetitive.
- Only one-tenth of 1 percent of DNA differs from one person to the next.

GM Crops

- The total acreage of GM crops worldwide is about 432 million acres (175 million ha).
- The United States has about 173 million acres (70 million ha) of GM crops, or about 40 percent of the world's total.

- At least 90 percent of the soy, cotton, canola, corn, and sugar beets sold in the United States have been genetically engineered.
- Regulatory agencies in fifty-nine countries have affirmed the safety of GM crops, approving 319 different GM traits in twenty-five crops.
- More than sixty countries around the world, including Australia, Japan, and all countries in the European Union, have significant restrictions or outright bans on the production and sale of GM crops.

Genetic Medicine

- There are more than six thousand known disorders caused by a mutation in a single gene.
- Genetic diseases occur in one out of every two hundred births.
- About 20 percent to 30 percent of all infant deaths are due to genetic disorders.
- Inherited genetic mutations play a role in about 5 percent to 10 percent of all cancers.
- According to the Gene Therapy Research Unit at the University of Sydney, 2,597 gene therapy clinical trials had been completed, were ongoing, or had been approved in thirty-eight countries as of November 2017.

Related Organizations and Websites

CDC Office of Public Health Genomics (OPHG)
1600 Clifton Rd.
Atlanta, GA 30329
website: www.cdc.gov

Part of the Centers for Disease Control and Prevention (CDC), a federal agency, the OPHG supports CDC programs, other federal agencies, and state health departments by identifying, evaluating, and implementing genomics practices to prevent and control the country's leading diseases. Its website includes Real Stories, Genetics 101, and a Weekly Update section on genomic medicine.

Debating Europe
website: www.debatingeurope.eu

Founded by the European University Institute, Debating Europe is a public platform designed to encourage debate about major issues confronting contemporary European society. The question for March 25, 2018, was, "Should GMOs be banned across Europe?" It includes two written and six video responses from European Parliament members representing seven political parties.

Genetics Home Reference
website: https://ghr.nlm.nih.gov

This National Institutes of Health website lists more than one thousand genetic health conditions, diseases, and syndromes. It also includes a guide to more than fourteen hundred genes. The gene description includes its normal function, health conditions related to genetic changes, and which chromosome it is located on, including a diagram showing its precise location.

Genome
website: http://genomemag.com

Written for the public at large, including patients, family, caregivers, and health care professionals, *Genome* offers in-depth stories about the people affected by chronic and life-altering diseases, as well as the efforts to use genetics to predict, prevent, diagnose, and treat those conditions.

National Cancer Institute
BG 9609 MSC 9760
9609 Medical Center Dr.
Bethesda, MD 20892
website: www.cancer.gov

One of the twenty-seven research institutes of the National Institutes of Health, the National Cancer Institute website includes an About Cancer section with a link to a Genetics page that includes information on genetic changes and cancer, hereditary cancer syndromes, and genetic tests for hereditary cancer syndromes.

National Genome Research Center (NGRC)
website: www.genome.gov

Founded in 1989 to carry out the role of the National Institutes of Health in the international Human Genome Project, the NGRC is a research institute dedicated to studying the genetic components of complex disorders. The NGRC website includes an education section with fact sheets on genetic science, research, and ethics.

Patient Privacy Rights
1006 Mopac Cir., Suite 102
Austin, TX 78746
website: https://patientprivacyrights.org

Patient Privacy Rights is a nonprofit organization dedicated to helping individuals realize their right to privacy through personal control of their health information—including genetic information—wherever such information is collected and used.

Virtual Genetics Education Centre, University of Leicester

website: www2.le.ac.uk

This easy-to-use website features simple menus, clear diagrams, and concise definitions to explain everything from what genetics is to genetics and ethics. The website also includes a glossary and links to outside resources.

For Further Research

Books

Toney Allman, *Genetics and Medicine*. San Diego: ReferencePoint, 2018.

David Bond, *Genetic Engineering*. Broomall, PA: Mason Crest, 2017.

Steven Monroe Lipkin, *The Age of Genomes: Tales from the Front Lines of Genetic Medicine*. Boston: Beacon, 2017.

Petra Miller, *Down Syndrome*. New York: Cavendish Square, 2016.

Megan Mitchell, *The Human Genome*. New York: Cavendish Square, 2016.

Internet Sources

Joan Conrow, "European Studies Disprove Seralini's GMO Maize Tumor Claims," Cornell Alliance for Science, June 7, 2018. https://alliancefor science.cornell.edu/blog/2018/06/european-studies-disprove-seralinis -gmo-maize-tumor-claims.

George Doe, "With Genetic Testing, I Gave My Parents the Gift of Divorce," Vox, September 9, 2014. www.vox.com/2014/9/9/5975653 /with-genetic-testing-i-gave-my-parents-the-gift-of-divorce-23andme.

Clyde Haberman, "Scientists Can Design 'Better' Babies. Should They?," *New York Times*, June 10, 2018. www.nytimes.com/2018/06/10/us/11 retro-baby-genetics.html?hp&action=click&pgtype=Homepage &clickSource=story-heading&module=second-column-region&region =top-news&WT.nav=top-news.

Justin Jouvenal et al., "Data on a Genealogy Site Led Police to the 'Golden State Killer' Suspect. Now Others Worry About a 'Treasure Trove of Data,'" *Washington Post*, April 27, 2018. www.washingtonpost.com /news/post-nation/wp/2018/04/27/data-on-a-genealogy-site-led-police

-to-the-golden-state-killer-suspect-now-others-worry-about-a-treasure
-trove-of-data/?utm_term=.455ad23a5785.

National Human Genome Research Institute, "Privacy in Genomics," April 21, 2015. www.genome.gov/27561246/privacy-in-genomics.

Deborah C. Peel, "The Hidden Danger of Do-It-Yourself Genetic Tests," *Newsweek*, March 7, 2017. www.newsweek.com/hidden-danger-do-it -yourself-genetic-tests-749475.

Laura Spinney, "We Don't Want to Know What Will Kill Us," *Slate*, September 29, 2017. www.slate.com/articles/health_and_science/medi cal_examiner/2017/09/genetic_testing_da.ta_reveals_the_irrationality _of_human_behavior.html.

Index

About the Author

Bradley Steffens is a poet, a novelist, and an award-winning author of more than forty nonfiction books for children and young adults.